SUCCESS

BUSINESS PLAN

Windshield Repair

ANDREW AJ WILSTHOLM

ISBN-10: 1482731118
ISBN-13: 978-1482731118

DEDICATION

Dedicated to my loving family, Kim, Emily and Addison

And to my
Dad,
Who's dreams and entrepreneurial heart, has enough power,
Motivation and inspiration for everyone.

DO NOT DUPLICATE OR DISTRIBUTE WITHOUT PERMISSION.

This presentation contains proprietary content and must not be duplicated or distributed without written permission. No portion of this material may be shared or reproduced in any manner under any circumstance whatsoever without advance written permission from Automotive Marketing Blueprint. No portion of this material is intended to offer legal, medical, personal or financial advice. We've taken every effort to ensure we accurately represent these strategies and their potential to help you grow your business. However, we do not purport this as a "get rich scheme" and there is no guarantee that you will earn any money using the content, strategies or techniques displayed here. Nothing in this presentation is a promise or guarantee of earnings. Your level of success in attaining similar results is dependent upon a number of factors including your skill, knowledge, ability, connections, dedication, business savvy, business focus, business goals, and financial situation. Because these factors differ according to individuals, we cannot guarantee your success, income level, or ability to earn revenue. You alone are responsible for your actions and results in life and business, and by your use of these materials, you agree not to attempt to hold us liable for any of your decisions, actions or results, at any time, under any circumstance. Any forward-looking statements outlined here are simply our expectations or forecasts for future potential, and thus are not guarantees or promises for actual performance. These statements are simply our opinion. The information contained herein cannot replace or substitute for the services of trained professionals in any field, including, but not limited to, financial or legal matters. Under no circumstances, including but not limited to negligence, will Andrew Wilstholm or Automotive Marketing Blueprint or any of its representatives or contractors be liable for any special or consequential damages that result from the use of, or the inability to use, the materials, information, or success strategies communicated through these materials, or any services following these materials, even if advised of the possibility of such damages.

For permissions requests, contact: Andrew Wilstholm at awilstholm@automotivemarketingblueprint.com

Automotive Marketing Blueprint www.automotivemarketingblueprint.com

CONTENTS

Introduction
Automotive Marketing Blueprint

Success Business Plan – For your Windshield Repair Business

Andrew Wilstholm

Congratulations on your purchase of a real Windshield Repair Business Plan that will help you create a strategic roadmap to grow your successful business. Making the decision is sometimes a hard one, but you have made the first and ultimate step to improving your success. As you read you will wonder if Acorn Auto Glass is real and the answer is yes but the real identity and location of the company is protected for obvious reasons.

I wrote this plan for an up coming company that needed some direction and to reduce potential failure. Although nothing is guaranteed, I wrote a plan that will keep them focused, on track and in business for years to come.

The great part is, you can spend as little or as much time as you need to tweak this plan to your needs, but you don't need to spend 100 hours or more crunching the data. You also don't need to learn and install new software. You now get to spend the time working on getting some business instead of spending a week of your life on the plan.

What Next? - How to edit this plan

I bet you are excited! Success Business Plan Template is an usable document that leads you through the central parts of your business plan, structured in a way that you can understand and lenders want to see.

First take a moment to print the document so you can see and feel the power of a plan. Read through the business plan to get a general feel and write down some notes and ideas on the side.

Additional research that you may need (not necessary) to fully complete this document is the population statistics for your area that you are planning to open your business. Also you may like to open the yellow pages to find a list of competitors in your trade and write them in the competitors section.

While you are there, note (or even photocopy) the competitors and the way they are selling their products. Who are successful and who are just doing ok? What are they saying? How can you be different? The yellow pages are also a good resource to start your list of companies you can offer your products to.

If you would like a copy of the word document, email the receipt to me and I will send you a copy for your editing. Other wise the process of typing it will help you own and remember the business plan. Open the word document on your computer (If you ordered it), and go through each page and re-edit the information to your goals and dreams. (Fix any spelling errors) Make yourself a logo and a tag line for the front page and any further customizations, then print and bind your success plan.

Periodically take the time (a few times a year) and read over the plan to see if you are on track and if you need to change anything. As a small business you can change and move quickly to get the best results for you.

I wish you the best of luck and ultimate success in your journey,

Andrew

1.0 Executive Summary

Introduction

Acorn Auto Glass (acornautoglass.com) creates a specialized experience for customers who need glass repaired. Acorn Auto Glass, Our strength being specialized service. In a market where service differentiation is difficult and no one really "wants" a windshield repair, marketing and USP (unique selling position) will ensure steady growth.

The focus of this business plan is to put forth objectives to solve the present cash-flow squeeze, increase client numbers, brand recognition and to increase profits from the present break-even level to net profits of $10,000 by the end of the first year. We intend to accomplish this by focusing on modifying our website, repackaging our more popular products, additional marketing tests and to concentrate on our designated target markets.

The Company

Acorn Auto Glass's mission is to make the auto glass experience and easy one and to provide exceptional service that leaves the client with a WOW factor, so that they can move on with their day. Acorn Auto Glass aims to provide fast, convenient service with the choice quality parts from the best suppliers in the world

Acorn Auto Glass is a limited liability corporation that is fully owned by one person, Mr. Andrew Wilstholm. Mr. Andrew Wilstholm comes from an auto glass background. The knowledge, experience, and contacts accumulated during that period have led to changes in the traditional modus operandi of Acorn Auto Glass.

At the present time, Acorn Auto Glass's facilities are all mobile based located in Lunenburg, Nova Scotia. There are currently less than ten employees at Acorn Auto Glass. The growth of the company will be determined by how accurately and efficiently the company is able to implement the facets of this business plan.

The Products

A general description of Acorn Auto Glass's core products would be Windshield Repairs. Windshield Repairs account for the focus and expertise of the Acorn Auto Glass model. Windshield repairs that are marketed and sold correctly can potentially outsell the replacement side. Side lites and back windows are an addition to the product line mostly as a pull strategy. Small side products we include for up sell and promotions are Aquapel and wiper sales.

The Market

There is a huge market in Nova Scotia for Auto Glass products, with plenty of profitable business to be had. Nearly 300 businesses have been identified as attractive in addition to those market sectors to which Acorn Auto Glass has directed its attention. Capturing market share at a profit is definitely achievable.

The company will refocus on a number of key industries that have a high level of consumption of our products. These include insurance companies, insurance agents, garages, mechanic shops, and auto suppliers, and fleet companies, institutions like funeral homes, doctors/dentists, travel agents, and Michelin and auto dealers. The use of specialty catalogues oriented strictly for these industries will be the tool to create greater market share.

Financial path to Success

With Acorn Auto Glass's refocus on its key industries and the creation of an effective website, the company expects its profits to steadily increase. Revenues are projected to increase by almost _____% over the next three years, from ~$__,000 to ~$___,000. We expect net profits will increase to $20,000 by year three. Such a large increase in profits is projected because we will be decreasing our marketing and advertising costs by a significant amount and increasing the efficiency of these activities. To implement our marketing changes and maintain sufficient cash, the company will be borrowing $5,000 this year in a short-term loan. Our projected cash flow will increase our cash balance and allow us to leverage this asset to creating new opportunities. During this time, we do not expect any difficulties in maintaining sufficient sales to meet our costs.

Chart: Highlights

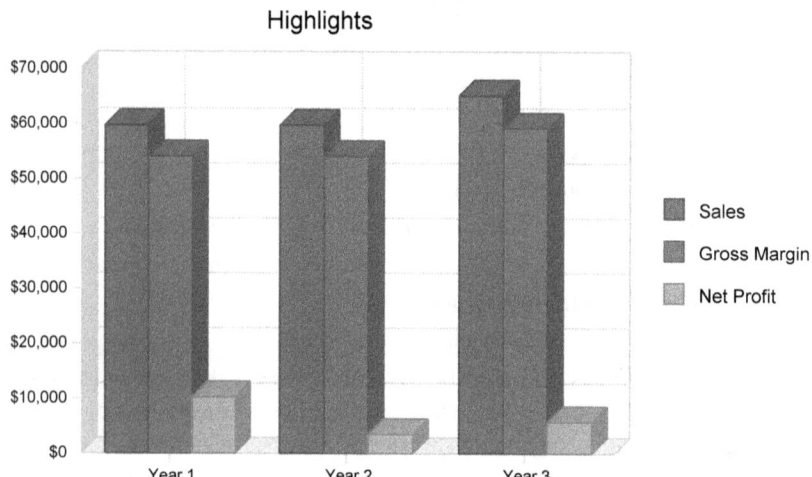

1.1 Objectives

There are five major objectives to this business plan, of which three are immediate and the fourth is of a longer-term nature:

1. Sales increase to $100,000 by end of second year and $125,000 by end of third year.
2. Increase the windshield repair unit sales
3. To increase the number of clients services by at least 20% per year through superior performance and word-of mouth referrals.
4. Re-focus owner Andrew Wilstholm, back to sales and marketing, and expanding workforce to 1-2 more people with mobile trucks
5. Become an established community destination by end of first year.

We also need to look at and define "What Qualifies Me to Succeed", what make me different?

1. Experience and time in trade
2. Experience in the skills set for Auto Glass
3. Likable
4. Great phone skills for closing the sale
5. Passion for the Trade
6. Looking to help people
7. Educated in Marketing and business
8. Educated in Human Resources

What are the Risk Mitigating steps for success (baby steps along the way as milestones to reducing risk of failure?)

1. Business Legal Setup
2. Banking set up
3. Business promotional materials
4. Truck/shop/workstation setup
5. Invoices produced and ready (paper or electronic)
6. Sales plan
7. Marketing plan
8. For-fill sales contracts
9. Build sales to _____ per month, _____-per year
10. Repeat, improve systems, evaluate methods and systems
11. Goals for next year

1.2 Mission

Acorn Auto Glass is devoted to quality, service and fair pricing in replacing and installing automotive glass and glass accessories. Making auto glass an easy experience plus ensuring fast, on time services for those in need is important.

1.3 Keys to Success

There are five generally accepted keys to success in the Auto Glass industry:

1. Personal sales and marketing (being remembered and noticed at time of need)
2. Segmentation of marketing to B2B and B2C
3. Quality & Timely work (Perceived and real)
4. Competitive but not cheep prices
5. Ideas and growth

Sales and marketing are keys to being in front of the customer when they need a glass part. Most Glass companies are not "top of mind" when ads are being advertised, but the moment a client needs service "familiar" companies get picked first.

Main advantage is our mobile service. Acorn Auto Glass makes it more convenient for consumers to have their glass repaired while at work or at home.

Competitive pricing is an issue and this is where marketing of service and product help. Supplier logistics and competitiveness help.

Capturing market share at a profit is definitely achievable if the above five steps are skillfully executed.

2.0 Company Analysis

Acorn Auto Glass has an effective hold on the market in the regional areas and after two years in the market place a firm customer base has been developed on the South Shore. Old marketing plans need to be re-evaluated and changes for growth need to happen are the two main reasons for spending the time and energy into a new/revised business plan. We are Comparing old ideals and projections with actual and using that knowledge to looking forward at the years to come.

This plan outlines the ideas and expertise in the automotive field and also has a plan to market and sell auto glass. Plans from zero dollars to 100,000 in sales are important to foresee in the next twelve months. This document is coupled with the Acorn Auto Glass IMC plan for full marketing impact.

By focusing on our strengths, our key customers, and the underlying values they need, Acorn Auto Glass will increase sales while also improving the gross margin on sales and cash management and working capital.

This business plan leads the way. It renews our vision and strategic focus: adding value to our target market segments, the Used and New Dealers and "Joe Blow" consumers, in our local market. It also provides the step-by-step plan for improving our sales, gross margin, and profitability.

This plan includes this summary, and chapters on the company, products and services, market focus, action plans and forecasts, management team, and financial plan.

2.1 Company Ownership

Acorn Auto Glass is a sole proprietorship, listed at the registry as "Acorn Auto Glass".

2.2 Start-up Summary

Our start-up costs come to $1650.00, which is mostly stationery, legal costs, and expenses associated with opening our first office. Costs may rise due to wants and needs. The start-up costs are to be financed by direct owner investment.

Table: Start-up

Start-up	
Requirements	
Start-up Expenses	
Legal	$200
Stationery etc.	$300
Insurance	$300

Rent	$100
Computer	$0
Other	$100
Cell Phone and Internet	$150
Total Start-up Expenses	$1,150
Start-up Assets	
Cash Required	$1,000
Other Current Assets	$0
Long-term Assets	$2,850
Total Assets	$3,850
Total Requirements	$5,000

Chart: Start-up

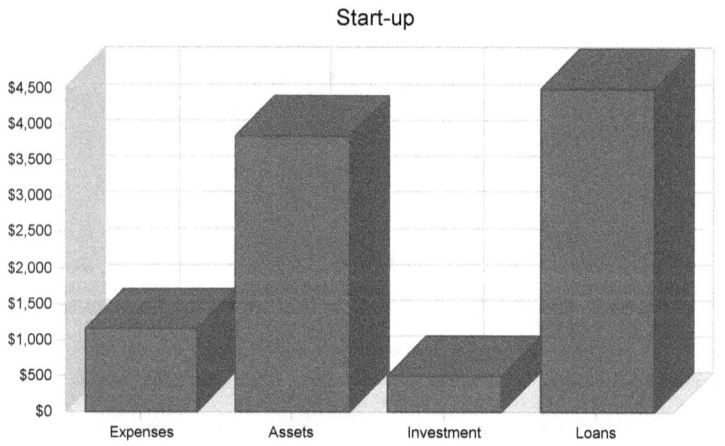

3.0 Products and Services

Acorn Auto Glass Product Lines (Segmentation)

Main Products include:

1. Windshield Repairs

2. Auto replacement Glass (Windshields or windshield commission referral)
3. Tempered glass (Side lites or commission referral)
4. Cosmetic auto accessories (Wipers, Vent visors, Aquapel)
5. Flat glass - Tempered, Safety and Plate (commission referral)

Industrial: Industrial customers include anyone who does service or contractual work for others, in addition to, Industrial clients also is authoritative referral source.

Consumer: Consumer customers include those who call on their own, public, use the internet or yellow pages to find a suitable service provider

4.0 Market Analysis

Market Analysis:

The overall market for Auto Glass products is immense. This business plan has identified between 20,000 and 30,000 vehicles that will be affected by glass damage. (35,000 homes may need glass as well)

The market tends to be confused with the glass industry but hangs onto what the "big" sellers advertise

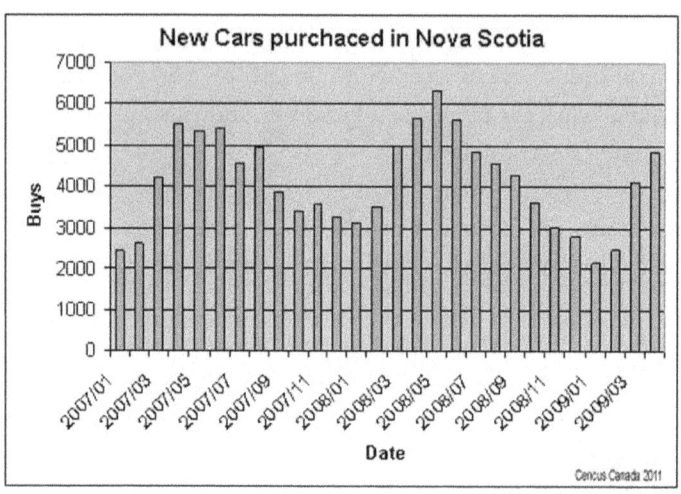

New Cars purchaced in Nova Scotia

Cencus Canada 2011

4.1 Market Segmentation

Demographic Segmentation

Our market segmentation scheme allows some room for estimates and nonspecific definitions. We focus on a small-medium level of business, and consumers.

Customers:

Acorn Auto Glass clients tend to radiate from Lunenburg outward to Hubbard's. Most clients reside in areas from Chester to the edge of Bridgewater. The Central of Bridgewater has not produced the volume of clients that was expected.

Who has bought service from Acorn Auto Glass?

1. Out of town clients
2. Males and females over 25 (own vehicle)
3. Mature Males and females
4. Client on the go
5. Cars Mostly older than 3 years old
6. Industrial and Fleet accounts

Potential clients can be broken down into four categories

1. Auto Dealers, Auto Repairers, and Mechanics -
2. Fleet companies - These include any company that has more than three vehicles.
3. Common Consumer - Joe Blow needs a glass and does not refer to his/her mechanic
4. Supplier - DIY - Supply only and intends on doing own work.
5. _____ (Add your thoughts)
6. _____

Geographic Segmentation -

Geographically the area of service covers east from exit 1-20 (East Point) to West -Yarmouth and North- into Kentville of Nova Scotia. Area segmentation includes towns of Bridgewater, Lunenburg, Mahone Bay, Chester, New Germany and Liverpool. Customers in towns tend to just call the company they always know.

(2006 Census of Population)

Table: Market Analysis

Market Analysis							
		Year 1	Year 2	Year 3	Year 4	Year 5	
Potential Customers	Growth						CAGR

Adults with Purchasing power who own a vehicle	10%	21,495	23,645	26,010	28,611	31,472	10.00%
Auto Dealers, Mechanics	5%	150	158	166	174	183	5.10%
Fleet Companies	5%	200	210	221	232	244	5.10%
Total	9.93%	21,845	24,013	26,397	29,017	31,899	9.93%

Chart: Market Analysis (Pie)

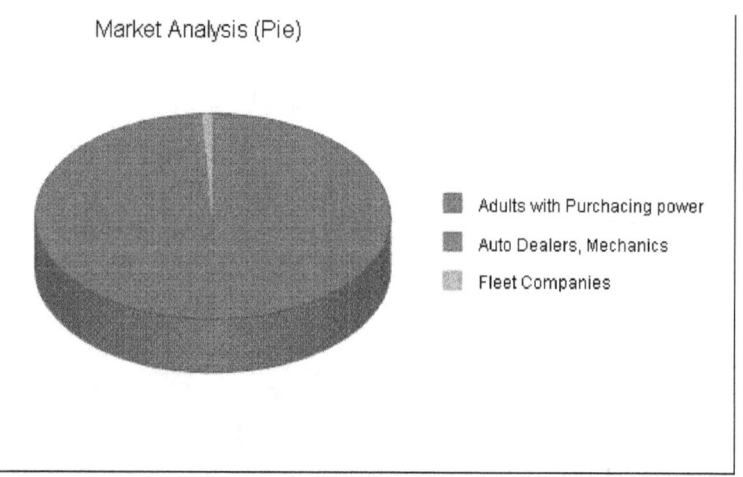

4.2 Target Market Segment Strategy

Auto Glass Target Market Segmentation

We have compiles a list of potential Industrial clients from Hubbard to Liverpool. The list is about 200 possibilities long.

1.   Public advertising includes Yellow pages
2.   A radio campaign is being considered to target and educate their loyal clients
3.   Promotional packages are also being considered to continually re-enforce current regular users of Scotia Glass

4.3 Industry Service Business Analysis

Auto Glass Market

(Ref: 1999, http://www.cb-bc.gc.ca/eic/site/cb-bc.nsf/eng/00811.html)

This is a competitive market in Canada with a number of chains and independents participating in most markets; there are over 3,000 glass shops whose main activity is the replacement and repair of auto glass and another 1,000 that do auto glass work on a part time basis.

This market is in transition in Canada because of various factors which have contributed to a reduction of the total market for auto glass, including:

•   the introduction by insurance companies of new auditing requirements and pre-work assessments carried out by a company's agent or nominee;
•   the reduced number of instances of replacement due to the introduction of lower costing repair technology;
•   the increase in volume discounts to insurance companies;
•   The rise in deductibles for glass coverage to $300 from $100 in Ontario.

As a result, prices for auto glass services have fallen in the past two years. We have no evidence that declining prices are the result of using lower quality materials.

No auto glass company singlehandedly or jointly dominates these markets and none would be able to dictate price increases above competitive levels because auto insurance companies, being the main purchaser of auto glass service, would prevent such a price increase by using their buying power. Another factor preventing significant price increases is that there are no significant barriers to entry in this industry; a large price increase would likely attract new entrants to the market that would restore lower prices.

Industry Overview (General Automotive)

The US auto repair shop industry includes about 170,000 firms with combined annual revenue of $90 billion. Large companies include Midas, Monro Muffler Brake, and Belron US. The industry is extremely fragmented the 50 largest companies hold less than 10 percent of the market. This industry generally includes quick oil change shops and car washes and excludes tire shops.

Competitive Landscape

Demand depends on car usage and the number of cars on the road. The profitability of individual companies depends on convenient location and good marketing. Large companies can maximize use of expensive diagnostic equipment and have advantages in purchasing, distribution, and marketing. Small companies can compete effectively by providing superior customer service or offering specialized services. The industry is labor-intensive: average annual revenue per worker is about $100,000.

Competition includes other venues that provide automotive services, including some gas stations, car dealerships, and branches of chain stores, like Sears and Kmart. Auto repair shops perform an estimated 70 percent of repairs for out-of-warranty vehicles, according to the Automotive Service Association (ASA). http://www.asashop.org/

Products, Operations & Technology

(This next section is quoted from Market Research Handbook, 2005, Reuters, 2006, so you don't loose the feel of the research you may need to do.)

About 70 percent of industry revenue comes from mechanical repair and 30 percent from collision repair. Mechanical jobs include repairs to undercar systems, (mufflers and exhausts, transmissions, brakes, and shock absorbers) or in underhood systems (engines, electrical systems, radiators). Body work includes exterior and interior repair and glass replacement. Other services include oil changes and car washes. Companies may sell parts for do-it-yourselfers (DIY).

The industry includes national and regional chains, franchises, and independent operators. The majority of auto repair shops are independently owned, although many are franchises of large companies. Car repair shops may specialize in a particular field of repair, such as brake jobs or collision repair, because of the specialized knowledge and equipment required. Most companies in the mechanical field provide generalized services, such as regular maintenance, in addition to specialty services.

In auto repair shops, estimators review vehicles and give customers quotes on the approximate cost of a repair. Estimators may rely on car makers' recommendations or computer software to help develop an accurate estimate. Repairs sometimes uncover other problems, resulting in additional work and charges in excess of the estimate. Regardless of the cause of error, inaccurate estimates have resulted in unhappy customers and general mistrust of the industry.

Mechanical repair shops deal mainly with deterioration of parts due to normal wear. Common repairs involve air conditioning, brake, transmission, and electrical systems. Because of the increased technological complexity of newer cars, most shops have specialized diagnostic equipment to identify and fix problems. Shops typically keep an inventory of replacement parts or have arrangements with quick delivery parts suppliers. Experienced, well-trained auto technicians are critical to quality repair work. Companies may also employ apprentice or entry-level technicians.

Collision repair involves two distinct types of repair: body work and painting (or refinishing). In the body shop, technicians correct damaged car frames and panels. Each repair is unique and depends on the accident that caused damage. The painting process includes several standard steps and operates more like an assembly line. Paint preparation includes feathering (smoothing the surface) and priming. Paint application typically involves applying multiple coats. Finishing provides a protective clear coat. Collision repair jobs usually take four to eight days. Equipment includes welders, paint booths, frame machines, and plasma cutters. Key staff includes framers, technicians, and painters.

A typical mechanical repair shop is 5,300 square feet and has seven service bays according to the Automotive Service Association (ASA). The number of repairs usually ranges from about 200 to 250 per month. A typical body shop is 12,000 square feet and has 17 service bays. Body shops average about 85 repairs per month.

Auto repair shops may buy replacement parts and supplies from full-line vendors, such as NAPA, or have supply arrangements with multiple distributors. Some large companies have purchasing contracts with specific suppliers. Chains of repair shops often maintain parts distribution centers to minimize the parts inventory needs at individual stores. With hundreds of parts needed for thousands of car models and production years, individual stores can't keep complete inventories. Shops may install OEM or aftermarket parts (rebuilt or not made by OEM company).

Many shops use computerized information systems to help manage point-of-sale, inventories, purchasing, accounting, and customer relations. Database programs give companies fast access to customer and vehicle information and repair histories. Electronic cataloging allows companies to research maintenance requirements and specific parts needed for a vehicle's particular make, model, and mileage. Diagnostic computer systems are essential equipment for mechanical repair shops because modern cars are filled with sensors and onboard diagnostics (OBD) - a vehicle's self-diagnostic system.

Many shops have websites that communicate basic information, including hours of operation and services performed. Some companies allow customers to schedule appointments or obtain estimates online.

More research can be found at-(Standard & Poor's, 2006). (Market Research Handbook, 2005, Reuters, 2006)

4.3.1 Competition and Buying Patterns

Competition

Two stores and four companies exist on the south shore now that include Apple, Speedy, D&B AG and Acorn Auto Glass. Market share would seem to not be in Speedy's hands although I would guess they have 35-40% market share. This is not confirmed. Consumers currently look up glass in the yellow pages and have only four choices and usually have to travel to Windsor to have the car serviced.

Speedy Auto Glass (Corporate Belron) (Previously Standard Auto Glass)

Managed by a current employee that does not seem to have the drive to capture new business

Was owned by John Smith and is a dying franchise with only 3 Standards in Atlantic Canada. They run 2 computer systems, one for glass and one for the rest of the operation. Probably half of their business comes from sales of car starters and audio equipment. Online the business is said to have 8 employees. My estimates are 3 for management, 2 glass guys, 2 starter techs and 1 floater for glass and stereos. They have one service truck

Apple Auto Glass

Is owned by Tim Wright.

Apples focus seems to be auto glass however they have a body shop as well.

1 service truck. Probably 8 employees. They rely on cutting price to attract clients when they don't have to. It would seem they depend on the body shop to help generate referrals from many sources.

Belron- Standard Auto Glass

Belron Company Description (Excerpt from their website – Belron.ca)

Source: http://www.hoovers.com/belron

Headquarters: 8288 Pie-IX Blvd.
Montreal, Quebec H1Z 3T6, Canada (Map) Belron Canada Company Description

When Canadian windshields get their bells rung, they can hope for help from Belron Canada. The company, a subsidiary of global glass repair leader Belron, provides both commercial and residential auto glass repair and replacement services through 390 stores and more than 40 distribution centers across Canada. Also assisting clients with their insurance claims, Belron Canada operates through several divisions, including Apple Auto Glass, Lebeau, Duro Vitres D'Autos, Speedy Glass, Standard Auto Glass (franchises), Vanfax (glass distribution), and Technicentre Plus (automotive electronics services).

Belron knows that glass can be all it's cracked up to be -- it's one of the world's largest auto glass repair and replacement companies. Belron is a holding company for around 25 auto-glass businesses (in about as many countries, including Australia, Canada, Germany, Turkey, the UK, and the US). Belron provides service around the clock, seven days a week, with technicians traveling to the customer, if needed. Belron companies additionally replace glass in buildings and sell glass wholesale. Belgian automotive firm D'Ieteren owns more than three-quarters of Belron.

Company Type Subsidiary of Belron - Main Headquarters
Fiscal Year-End December
2008 Sales (mil.) $198.7
2008 Employees 1,700
Service Centers 380

5.0 Web Plan Analysis

The Acorn Auto Glass website will be the virtual business card and portfolio for the company, as well as its online "home." The Acorn Auto Glass website needs to be a simple, yet elegant and well designed, website that stays current with the latest trends and provides information to the customers and a portal to our programs and products. A site that is too flashy, or tries to use too much of the latest Shockwave of Flash technology can be overdone, and cause potential clients to look elsewhere for products or information.

5.1 Website Marketing Strategy

Website marketing strategy can come in a few forms.

Our focus this year will be client education and contact info such as phone number, location of service. Developing a client list is also on the horizon and should be completed this year.

Facebook home and landing pages will be made and regular posts about glass and promotions

Twitter - have an account set up

5.2 Web Development Requirements

The Acorn Auto Glass website will be initially developed with few technical resources. A simple hosting provider, Ironbound ebusiness web hosting services, will host the site and provide the technical back end.

Acorn Auto Glass will work with an Ironbound Marketing and associates, a Nova Scotia based user graphic and interface designer to develop the simple, elegant, yet Internet focused site. This group will design all website graphics and layout.

The maintenance of the site will be done by Ironbound eMarketing and associates. As the website rolls out future development such as newsletters and other related auto glass related issues, a technical resource may need to be contracted to build the tractable download and the newsletter capabilities.

6.0 Strategy and Implementation Summary

We have clearly defined the target market and have differentiated ourselves by offering a unique solution to our customers information needs. Our sales and marketing strategy will be a combination of targeted mass marketing techniques as well as a focused direct sales team approach. Reasonable sales targets have been established with an implementation plan designed to ensure the goals set forth below are achieved.

Emphasize Customer Service

Acorn Auto Glass will differentiate themselves from other auto glass care facilities. We will establish our business offering as a clear and viable alternative for our target market.

Build a Relationship-Oriented Business

Build long-term relationships with clients, not just an occasional visit. Let them become dependent on Acorn Auto Glass to help out in many situations. Make them understand the value of the relationship.

Focus on Target Markets

We need to focus our offerings on the busy professionals, who want to save time to enjoy convenience, multiple services, and total satisfaction of services.

Differentiate and Fulfill the Promise

We can't just market and sell service and products; we must actually deliver as well. We need to make sure we have the knowledge-intensive business and service-intensive business we claim to have.

6.1 SWOT Analysis

The SWOT analysis provides us with an opportunity to examine the internal strengths and weaknesses Acorn Auto Glass must address. It also allows us to examine the opportunities presented to Acorn Auto Glass as well as potential threats.

Acorn Auto Glass has a valuable inventory of strengths that will help it succeed. These strengths include: a knowledgeable and friendly staff, state-of-the-art Mobile Trucks, and a clear vision of the market need. Strengths are valuable, but it is also important to realize the weaknesses Acorn Auto Glass must address. These weaknesses include: a dependence on dependence on Insurance Companies, and the cost factors associated advertising. Somewhere in all of this we need to address that almost everyone doesn't want a repair or replacement, they only need one when it happens to them. Repeat sales are at only 10% which means it almost never happens to them again.

Acorn Auto Glass strengths will help it capitalize on emerging opportunities. These opportunities include, but are not limited to, a growing population of daily Internet users, and the growing social bonds fostered by networking. Threats that Acorn Auto Glass should be aware of include, the rapidly rising cost of advertising, and re-emerging local competitors.

6.1.1 Strengths

1. Knowledgeable and friendly staff (As a Region). We've gone to great lengths at Acorn Auto Glass to find people with a passion for Repairing and helping clients with their auto glass needs. Our staff is both knowledgeable and eager to please.
2. State-of-the art equipment. Part of the Acorn Auto Glass experience includes access to state-of-the-art Auto Glass equipment. Our customers enjoy trust that they are in good hands.
3. Site ambiance. When you walk on site of Acorn Auto Glass, you'll feel the expertise of the installer and know he has the best tools to complete the job.
4. Clear vision of the market need. Acorn Auto Glass knows what it takes to build an up-to-date auto glass business. We know the customers, we know the technology of glass, and we know how to build the service that will bring the two together.

6.1.2 Weaknesses

1. A dependence on Insurance Companies. Acorn Auto Glass is a small company with the very small footprint in the market. Cultivating and nurturing the public and insurance agents with the trust and type of quality work we do, is a challenging task. Steering from the main Auto glass Giants further thwarts our effort in generating new clients.
2. Cost factor associated with advertising. Advertising appears to be for the giants of the auto glass world. Creating an effective radio campaign will be about $8-$10 thousand dollars and effective newspaper ads generate costs into $3-$7000 for an effective campaign. Creativity is key and using mediums no one else is using is a great idea, but time is a constraint. Money is only made when a windshield is repaired.
3. Cost factor in attracting new employees. Glass employees need to be intelligent enough to process and do the job but no so ambitious to eventually open on their own. Suppose this is an

issue at all companies. Finding a way to reward and satisfy employees for retention is important. Costs are high to train new people for replacement and reasonable for Windshield Repairs.

6.1.3 Opportunities

1. Sales and relationships. The big guys fall short in this way at this time. Everybody wants to by from someone they know. Aggressiveness in this area really pays off.
2. Networking with others. Making more events and upscale lunches
3. Advertising. Finding the funds to advertise effectively. List the types of medium to go after. Check the Guerrilla marketing manual
4. Internet. Website improvement

6.1.4 Threats

1. Rapidly rising costs of fuel and glass prices. The cost of fuel effects everyone in the industry
2. Emerging strength of the big guys. Currently, Acorn Auto Glass is enjoying a target market advantage in the local market. However, marketing powers and big dollars are a possibility from the big guys. (Belron) and we need to be prepared for their re-entry into the market. Many of our programs will be designed to build customer loyalty, and it is our hope that our quality service and won't be easily duplicated.

6.2 Competitive Edge

The advantages Acorn Auto Glass has over the competition are numerous:

- Acorn Auto Glass will have excellent locations to serve clients fast
- Acorn Auto Glass has a strategic dedicated mobile service for winter
- Acorn Auto Glass has the ability to adjust to prices
- Acorn Auto Glass has the ability to purchase from several providers

6.3 Marketing Strategy

The marketing strategy is the core of the main strategy:

1. Emphasize service and support.
2. Build a relationship business.
3. Focus on small business and high-end home office as key target markets.

6.4 Sales Strategy

Sales is a step process that intertwines with the marketing efforts

1. A sales target list will be made from the yellow pages
2. The names will be broken into territories and profile to create efficiency in seeing prospects and to better establish a routine.
3. Business cards and flyers are the main venue to give away to folks and create discussion.
4. Face to face sales will account for 80% of the initial jobs in the first 6 months to a year.
5. Personal sales coupled with marketing efforts (yellow pages, newspaper ads, flyers, Radio) will create the "call", after that it is up to me to talk/sell the prospect into getting the job done.
6. Cold phone sales account for a percentage of new business and I would like to "script" to introduce myself and ask if they need anything. Implementing this would be a bonus
7. The "Call" is an art, since this is just one step in getting the job.
8. "Thank you for calling Acorn Auto Glass, How may I help you?"
    o Price?
    o Any quotes yet?

Closing sales prospects?

Thank you for calling _____auto glass. You have reached the Voicemail for _____, and your call is very important to me.

Please leave your name, phone number, and any vehicle details, and I will call you back as soon as possible. Thank you and have a great day

Common Windshield Rejections

Realize these are the worst case scenario and that most people are receptive to having their windshield inspected. The general population is very aware of free repairs and the significance of the structural strength of the windshield; however, they like to test your knowledge on the topic. Top sale people use this material and repeat everyday and consistently earn top dollars. Get comfortable approaching people or settle for less.

I just checked and we don't have any rock chips.

Oh really? That's perfect it's always good to be on top of those things. We were actually just talking about that the other day with (insert personal experience) and they had thought they checked but it turned out that there was one in the tinted area around the outside of the windshield, it spread and eventually had to be replaced. I'll just give the glass a quick inspection so you know for sure.

We were just at Crazy lube and they always check.

Perfect. Those guys at jiffy lube are always pretty vigilant when it comes to your engine, did the same guys that checked your oil check your glass because a lot of those jiffy lube places just send their lube guys to give the cars a check, the problem is that they are not actually certified. No worries though, it'll just take me a second to give the glass an inspection. Are any of these cars out here on the street yours?

I have a guy that fixes mine for me.

That's great! Its good to stay on top of these kinds of things, those chips are like late fees, before you know it you're forking out $200 for something that should have been free. I'll just take a quick follow up look and if there is a chip I'll call your guy and give him the details. Are these your vehicles here in the driveway?

My husband takes care of all the "car" stuff.

Okay is He really meticulous about the little details. If they're at all the same there's nothing more upsetting than having a chip spread on you before you get a chance to fix it. Why don't I just give the windshield a quick inspection and if there's anything array we'll go from there, did you park any of them outside?

Maneuver price, delivery, and conditions

Competitiveness comes from $20 over highest cost (Try for more after a few months) Depending on the month and the landscape prices may drop to $10- $15 dollars over cost. At that moment you have to decide if you just want the job. Taking the job means the competitors price gouge didn't work and they will have to find other reasonable methods to attract the job. Sometimes not taking the job means they win and look good to the client. Is the job worth it or is it worth it?

6.4.1 Sales Forecast

Sales forecasts happen with only one employee (Andrew Wilstholm). One way to increase sales is to have another repair person.

Action plan

1. Seek out helper for days I cannot be there
2. Make sure I'm not neglecting clients
3. Grab promotional materials and visit potential clients

Table: Sales Forecast

Sales Forecast			
	Year 1	Year 2	Year 3
Unit Sales			
Windshield Replacement	0	0	0
Windshield Repair	720	720	780
Tempered Glass (Back and Side)	0	0	0
Safety Glass And Plate Glass	0	0	0
Wipers	81	81	90
Aquapel	26	26	60
Thermo Units	0	0	0
Heavy Equipment Glass	0	0	0
Ship Glass Industrial	0	0	0
Windshield Remove and Replace (Re/Re)	0	0	0
Total Unit Sales	827	827	930
Unit Prices	Year 1	Year 2	Year 3
Windshield Replacement	$0.00	$0.00	$0.00
Windshield Repair	$80.00	$80.00	$80.00
Tempered Glass (Back and Side)	$0.00	$0.00	$0.00
Safety Glass And Plate Glass	$0.00	$0.00	$0.00
Wipers	$18.00	$18.00	$18.00
Aquapel	$20.00	$20.00	$20.00
Thermo Units	$0.00	$0.00	$0.00
Heavy Equipment Glass	$0.00	$0.00	$0.00
Ship Glass Industrial	$0.00	$0.00	$0.00
Windshield Remove and Replace (Re/Re)	$0.00	$0.00	$0.00

Sales

Windshield Replacement	$0	$0	$0
Windshield Repair	$57,600	$57,600	$62,400
Tempered Glass (Back and Side)	$0	$0	$0
Safety Glass And Plate Glass	$0	$0	$0
Wipers	$1,458	$1,458	$1,620
Aquapel	$520	$520	$1,200
Thermo Units	$0	$0	$0
Heavy Equipment Glass	$0	$0	$0
Ship Glass Industrial	$0	$0	$0
Windshield Remove and Replace (Re/Re)	$0	$0	$0
Total Sales	$59,578	$59,578	$65,220

Direct Unit Costs	Year 1	Year 2	Year 3
Windshield Replacement	$0.00	$0.00	$0.00
Windshield Repair	$6.40	$6.40	$6.40
Tempered Glass (Back and Side)	$0.00	$0.00	$0.00
Safety Glass And Plate Glass	$0.00	$0.00	$0.00
Wipers	$7.20	$7.20	$7.20
Aquapel	$2.00	$2.00	$2.00
Thermo Units	$0.00	$0.00	$0.00
Heavy Equipment Glass	$0.00	$0.00	$0.00
Ship Glass Industrial	$0.00	$0.00	$0.00
Windshield Remove and Replace (Re/Re)	$0.00	$0.00	$0.00

Direct Cost of Sales

Windshield Replacement	$0	$0	$0
Windshield Repair	$4,608	$4,608	$4,992
Tempered Glass (Back and Side)	$0	$0	$0
Safety Glass And Plate Glass	$0	$0	$0
Wipers	$583	$583	$648
Aquapel	$52	$52	$120
Thermo Units	$0	$0	$0
Heavy Equipment Glass	$0	$0	$0

Ship Glass Industrial Windshield Remove and Replace (Re/Re)	$0 $0	$0 $0	$0 $0
Subtotal Direct Cost of Sales	$5,243	$5,243	$5,760

Chart: Sales Monthly

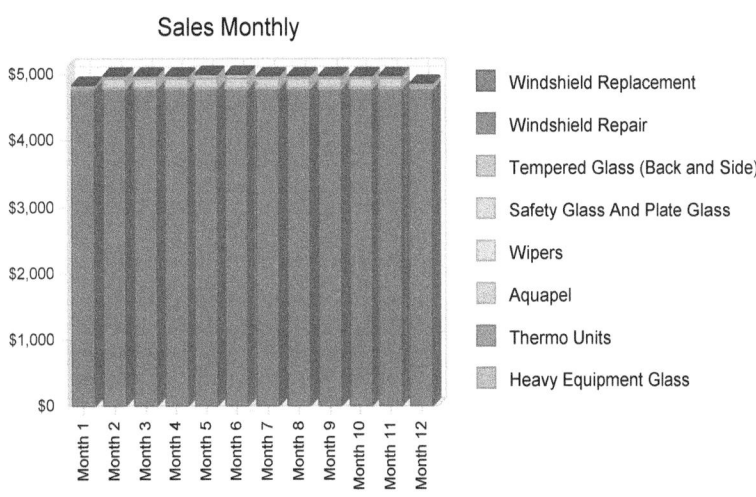

Chart: Sales by Year

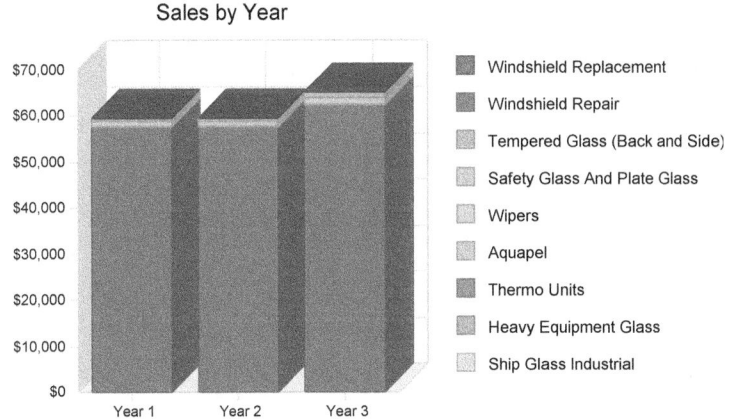

6.5 Milestones

The following table lists important program milestones, with dates and managers in charge, and budgets for each. The milestone schedule indicates our emphasis on planning for implementation.

7.0 Management Summary

Our management philosophy is simple and is an integral part of our values: doing right things right, the first time (Kina'ole).

Acorn Auto Glass will be an employee-owned company and we all share the same vision of providing our clients (who in many cases are friends and neighbors) with the very best in customer service - period. We will encourage personal growth, creativity, and enable individual empowerment to achieve this goal. We will manage the business by setting achievable Balanced Scorecard goals, measuring them, and making mid-stream adjustments as necessary.

7.1 Personnel Plan

The Personnel Plan reflects the staffing levels required to create the growing mobile service, marketing, sales, and establish the customer base needed to achieve the revenues projected and reach profitability.

We have projected a staff of 2 employees by June 2013 and recognize the need to increase the sales/marketing department in 2014. The new sales/marketing positions have not been included in this plan.

8.0 Financial Plan

The following is the Acorn Auto Glass financial plan.

Although we are treating the business as a start-up company, the financial plan is solidly based on past performance. We have taken actual Acorn Auto Glass income and expenses from the past three years, and eliminated corporate overhead expenses. We then projected income based on actual past performance.

We approached the financial planning from a conservative standpoint, and based those numbers on achievable gross margins. Also, our actual interest and tax rates will most likely be lower than the assumed rates due to our being structured as an employee-owned corporation.

8.1 Start-up Funding

Acorn Auto Glass, LLC start-up costs are detailed above, in the Start-up Table. The following table shows how these start-up costs will be funded by owner and investor capital.

Start-up Funding	
Start-up Expenses to Fund	$1,150
Start-up Assets to Fund	$3,850
Total Funding Required	$5,000
Assets	
Non-cash Assets from Start-up	$2,850
Cash Requirements from Start-up	$1,000
Additional Cash Raised	$0
Cash Balance on Starting Date	$1,000
Total Assets	$3,850
Liabilities and Capital	
Liabilities	
Current Borrowing	$1,000
Long-term Liabilities	$2,500
Accounts Payable (Outstanding Bills)	$800
Other Current Liabilities (interest-free)	$200
Total Liabilities	$4,500

Capital	
Planned Investment	
Owner	$250
Investor	$250
Additional Investment Requirement	$0
Total Planned Investment	$500
Loss at Start-up (Start-up Expenses)	($1,150)
Total Capital	($650)
Total Capital and Liabilities	$3,850
Total Funding	$5,000

8.2 Important Assumptions

The table below presents the assumptions used in the financial calculations of this business plan.

8.3 Break-even Analysis

For our break-even analysis, we assume running costs of approximately $_____per month, which includes our full payroll, rent, and utilities, and an estimation of other running costs.

Table: Break-even Analysis

Break-even Analysis	

Monthly Units Break-even	50
Monthly Revenue Break-even	$3,586
Assumptions:	
Average Per-Unit Revenue	$72.04
Average Per-Unit Variable Cost	$6.34
Estimated Monthly Fixed Cost	$3,270

Chart: Break-even Analysis

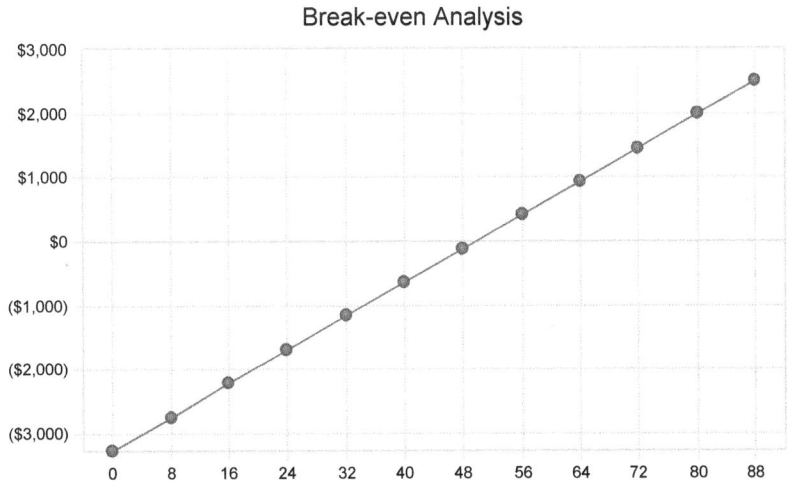

8.4 Projected Profit and Loss

The Profit and Loss table is summed up below:

- Rent: IN THE CHART - will try to find a location not to pay, but a great location can be the difference
- Depreciation: Truck, tent, signage and equipment
- Contract Labor: One contract laborer works at $11/hour (30 hrs weekly) = $1430 per month, plus commission
- Utilities:
- Telephone: Cell phone at $100 per month Insurance:
- Leased Vehicles: non
- Internet Services: The Company pays $22.50 monthly to Ironbound for Internet connection and $75 monthly for Web hosting. Total monthly Internet services come to $197.50.
- Postage: Normal postage (does not include special promotional mailings) will cost approximately $___ per month.

Our Pro Forma Profit and Loss statement was constructed from a conservative point-of-view, and is based in large part on past performance. By strengthening our service position, and rebuilding our customer relationships, we will widen our customer base and increase sales.

Month-to-month assumptions for profit and loss are included in the appendix.

Table: Profit and Loss

Pro Forma Profit and Loss			
	Year 1	Year 2	Year 3
Sales	$59,578	$59,578	$65,220
Direct Cost of Sales	$5,243	$5,243	$5,760

Other Costs of Sales	$200	$200	$200
Total Cost of Sales	$5,443	$5,443	$5,960
Gross Margin	$54,135	$54,135	$59,260
Gross Margin %	90.86%	90.86%	90.86%
Expenses			
Payroll	$19,200	$25,000	$26,000
Marketing/Promotion	$3,950	$4,500	$5,000
Depreciation	$300	$300	$200
Rent	$3,500	$3,500	$3,500
Utilities	$1,200	$1,200	$1,200
Insurance	$3,600	$3,700	$3,750
Payroll Taxes	$2,880	$3,285	$3,500
Other	$710	$700	$700
Vehicle and Fuel	$2,700	$3,300	$3,400
Phone and Internet	$1,200	$3,600	$3,600
Total Operating Expenses	$39,240	$49,085	$50,850
Profit Before Interest and Taxes	$14,895	$5,050	$8,410
EBITDA	$15,195	$5,350	$8,610
Interest Expense	$318	$284	$262
Taxes Incurred	$4,373	$1,430	$2,444
Net Profit	$10,204	$3,336	$5,704
Net Profit/Sales	17.13%	5.60%	8.75%

Chart: Profit Monthly

Profit Monthly

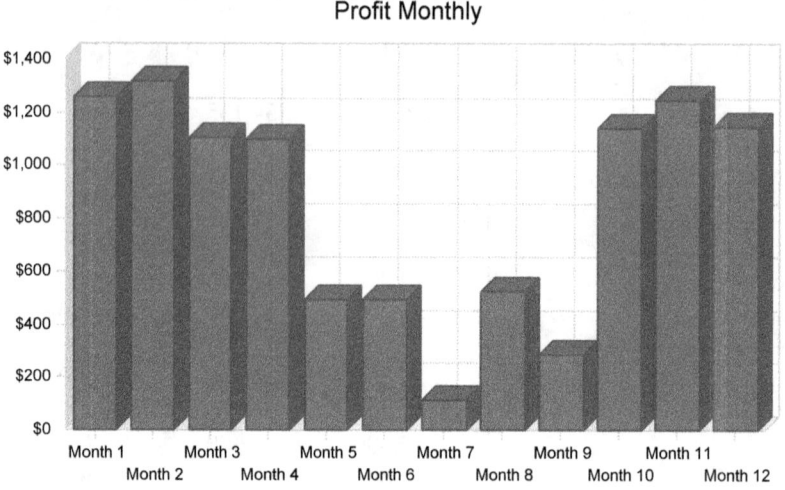

Chart: Profit Yearly

Profit Yearly

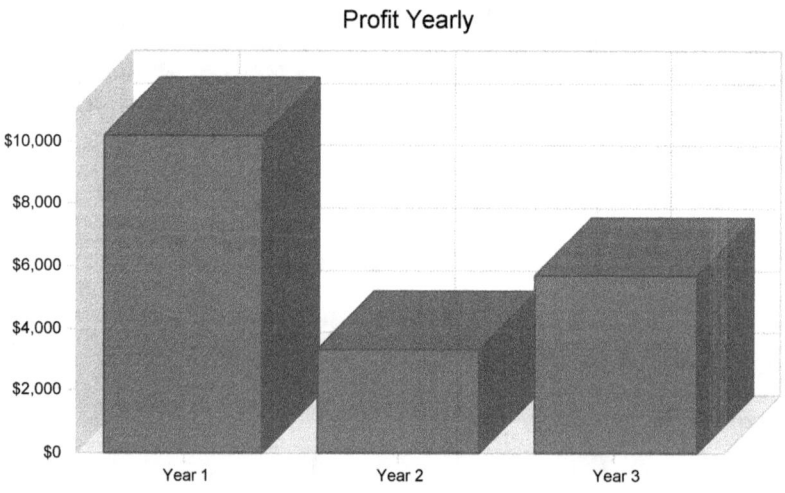

Chart: Gross Margin Monthly

Gross Margin Monthly

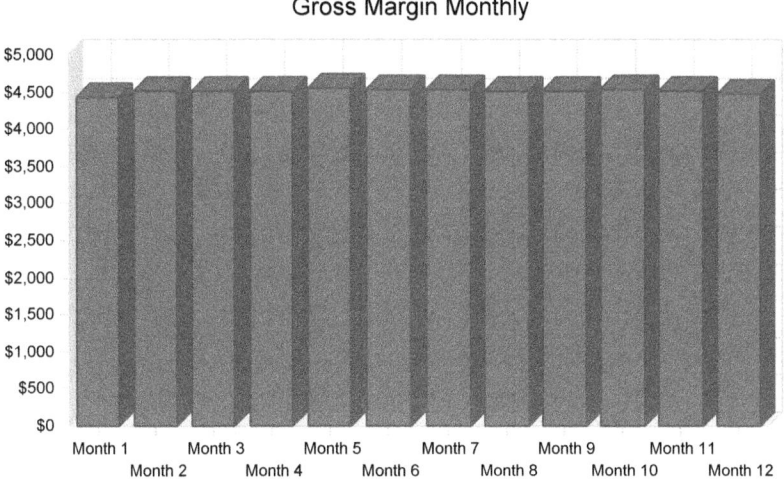

Chart: Gross Margin Yearly

Gross Margin Yearly

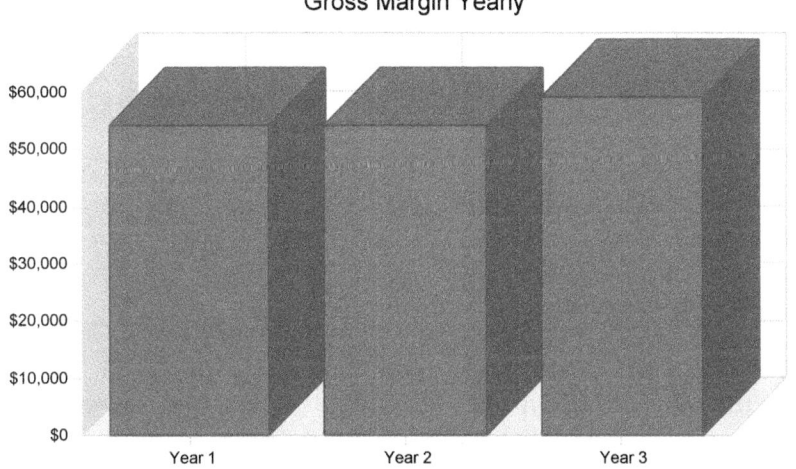

8.5 Projected Cash Flow

The cash flow depends on assumptions for inventory turnover, payment days, and accounts receivable management. Our projected 60-day collection days are not ideal, but it is realistic in this market, and hard for us to effectively change. We're better off planning for it than ignoring it. We need significant new financing in March to get through a cash flow dip as we build up for mid-year sales.

Table: Cash Flow

Pro Forma Cash Flow			
	Year 1	Year 2	Year 3
Cash Received			
Cash from Operations			
Cash Sales	$44,684	$44,684	$48,915
Cash from Receivables	$13,099	$14,895	$16,135
Subtotal Cash from Operations	$57,782	$59,578	$65,050
Additional Cash Received			
Sales Tax, VAT, HST/GST Received	$3,575	$3,575	$3,913
New Current Borrowing	$0	$0	$0
New Other Liabilities (interest-free)	$12,200	$0	$0
New Long-term Liabilities	$0	$0	$0
Sales of Other Current Assets	$0	$0	$0
Sales of Long-term Assets	$0	$0	$0
New Investment Received	$0	$0	$0
Subtotal Cash Received	$73,557	$63,153	$68,963
Expenditures	Year 1	Year 2	Year 3
Expenditures from Operations			
Cash Spending	$19,200	$25,000	$26,000
Bill Payments	$28,267	$30,806	$33,121

Subtotal Spent on Operations	$47,467	$55,806	$59,121
Additional Cash Spent			
Sales Tax, VAT, HST/GST Paid Out	$3,575	$3,575	$3,913
Principal Repayment of Current Borrowing	$550	$20	$20
Other Liabilities Principal Repayment	$25	$50	$50
Long-term Liabilities Principal Repayment	$0	$200	$200
Purchase Other Current Assets	$50	$50	$50
Purchase Long-term Assets	$0	$0	$0
Dividends	$0	$0	$0
Subtotal Cash Spent	$51,667	$59,700	$63,354
Net Cash Flow	$21,890	$3,452	$5,609
Cash Balance	$22,890	$26,342	$31,951

Chart: Cash

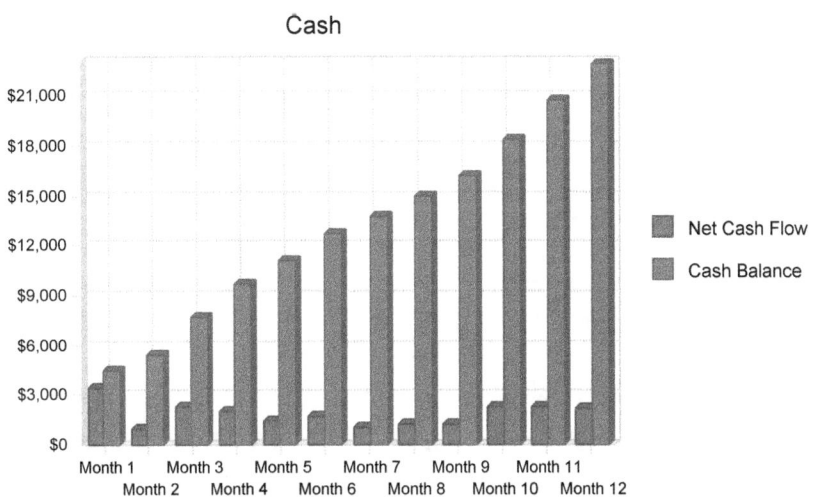

8.6 Projected Balance Sheet

The Projected Balance Sheet is quite solid. We do not project any real trouble meeting our debt obligations--as long as we can achieve our specific objectives.

Table: Balance Sheet

Pro Forma Balance Sheet			
	Year 1	Year 2	Year 3
Assets			
Current Assets			
Cash	$22,890	$26,342	$31,951
Accounts Receivable	$1,796	$1,796	$1,966
Other Current Assets	$50	$100	$150
Total Current Assets	$24,736	$28,238	$34,067
Long-term Assets			
Long-term Assets	$2,850	$2,850	$2,850
Accumulated Depreciation	$300	$600	$800
Total Long-term Assets	$2,550	$2,250	$2,050
Total Assets	$27,286	$30,488	$36,117
Liabilities and Capital	Year 1	Year 2	Year 3
Current Liabilities			
Accounts Payable	$2,407	$2,543	$2,738
Current Borrowing	$450	$430	$410
Other Current Liabilities	$12,375	$12,325	$12,275
Subtotal Current	$15,232	$15,298	$15,423

Liabilities			
Long-term Liabilities	$2,500	$2,300	$2,100
Total Liabilities	$17,732	$17,598	$17,523
Paid-in Capital	$500	$500	$500
Retained Earnings	($1,150)	$9,054	$12,390
Earnings	$10,204	$3,336	$5,704
Total Capital	$9,554	$12,890	$18,593
Total Liabilities and Capital	$27,286	$30,488	$36,117
Net Worth	$9,554	$12,890	$18,593

8.7 Business Ratios

The table below presents common business ratios as a reference. Industry Profile comparisons are excluded from this table since the business of "cargo tracking" does not fall underneath any predefined Industry dataset.

Editor's Note: SIC code needs to be accessed for viewing in sample plan browser. We chose SIC 7536, (NAICS 811122) Windshields and Automotive Glass (Automotive Glass Replacement Shops), as the closest option.

Alternate Industries (NAICS): 238150 - Glass and Glazing Contractors

Table: Ratios

Ratio Analysis				
	Year 1	Year 2	Year 3	Industry Profile
Sales Growth	n.a.	0.00%	9.47%	-3.05%
Percent of Total Assets				
Accounts Receivable	6.58%	5.89%	5.44%	12.28%
Other Current Assets	0.18%	0.33%	0.42%	36.14%
Total Current Assets	90.65%	92.62%	94.32%	61.83%
Long-term Assets	9.35%	7.38%	5.68%	38.17%
Total Assets	100.00%	100.00%	100.00%	100.00%
Current Liabilities	55.82%	50.18%	42.70%	30.66%
Long-term Liabilities	9.16%	7.54%	5.81%	58.05%
Total Liabilities	64.99%	57.72%	48.52%	88.70%
Net Worth	35.01%	42.28%	51.48%	11.30%

Percent of Sales				
Sales	100.00%	100.00%	100.00%	100.00%
Gross Margin	90.86%	90.86%	90.86%	53.42%
Selling, General & Administrative Expenses	73.74%	85.26%	82.12%	22.29%
Advertising Expenses	6.63%	7.55%	7.67%	1.36%
Profit Before Interest and Taxes	25.00%	8.48%	12.89%	6.01%
Main Ratios				
Current	1.62	1.85	2.21	1.53
Quick	1.62	1.85	2.21	1.09
Total Debt to Total Assets	64.99%	57.72%	48.52%	88.70%
Pre-tax Return on Net Worth	152.58%	36.97%	43.82%	245.85%
Pre-tax Return on Assets	53.42%	15.63%	22.56%	27.77%
Additional Ratios	Year 1	Year 2	Year 3	
Net Profit Margin	17.13%	5.60%	8.75%	n.a
Return on Equity	106.80%	25.88%	30.68%	n.a
Activity Ratios				
Accounts Receivable Turnover	8.29	8.29	8.29	n.a
Collection Days	43	44	42	n.a
Accounts Payable Turnover	12.41	12.17	12.17	n.a
Payment Days	28	29	29	n.a
Total Asset Turnover	2.18	1.95	1.81	n.a
Debt Ratios				
Debt to Net Worth	1.86	1.37	0.94	n.a
Current Liab. to Liab.	0.86	0.87	0.88	n.a
Liquidity Ratios				
Net Working	$9,504	$12,940	$18,643	n.a

Capital				
Interest Coverage	46.85	17.78	32.10	n.a
Additional Ratios				
Assets to Sales	0.46	0.51	0.55	n.a
Current Debt/Total Assets	56%	50%	43%	n.a
Acid Test	1.51	1.73	2.08	n.a
Sales/Net Worth	6.24	4.62	3.51	n.a
Dividend Payout	0.00	0.00	0.00	n.a

Notes:

Appendix   Table: Sales Forecast

Sales Forecast	Month 1	Month 2	Month 3	Month 4	Month 5	Month 6	Month 7	Month 8	Month 9	Month 10	Month 11	Month 12
Unit Sales												
Windshield Replacement	0	0	0	0	0	0	0	0	0	0	0	0
Windshield Repair	60	60	60	60	60	60	60	60	60	60	60	60
Tempered Glass (Back and Side)	0	0	0	0	0	0	0	0	0	0	0	0
Safety Glass And Plate Glass	0	0	0	0	0	0	0	0	0	0	0	0
Wipers	0	8	8	8	8	8	8	8	8	8	8	1
Aquapel	2	2	2	2	3	3	2	2	2	2	2	2
Thermo	0	0	0	0	0	0	0	0	0	0	0	0

Units	Month 1	Month 2	Month 3	Month 4	Month 5	Month 6	Month 7	Month 8	Month 9	Month 10	Month 11	Month 12
Heavy Equipment Glass	0	0	0	0	0	0	0	0	0	0	0	0
Ship Glass	0	0	0	0	0	0	0	0	0	0	0	0
Industrial	0	0	0	0	0	0	0	0	0	0	0	0
Windshield Remove and Replace (Re/Re)	0	0	0	0	0	0	0	0	0	0	0	0
Total Unit Sales	62	70	70	70	71	71	70	70	70	70	70	63

Unit Prices	Month 1	Month 2	Month 3	Month 4	Month 5	Month 6	Month 7	Month 8	Month 9	Month 10	Month 11	Month 12
Windshield Replacement	$200.00	$200.00	$200.00	$200.00	$200.00	$200.00	$200.00	$200.00	$200.00	$200.00	$200.00	$200.00
Windshield Repair	$80.00	$80.00	$80.00	$80.00	$80.00	$80.00	$80.00	$80.00	$80.00	$80.00	$80.00	$80.00
Tempered Glass	$150.00	$150.00	$150.00	$150.00	$150.00	$150.00	$150.00	$150.00	$150.00	$150.00	$150.00	$150.00

(Back and Side)												
Safety Glass And Plate Glass	$100.00	$100.00	$100.00	$100.00	$100.00	$100.00	$100.00	$100.00	$100.00	$100.00	$100.00	$100.00
Wipers	$18.00	$18.00	$18.00	$18.00	$18.00	$18.00	$18.00	$18.00	$18.00	$18.00	$18.00	$18.00
Aquapel	$20.00	$20.00	$20.00	$20.00	$20.00	$20.00	$20.00	$20.00	$20.00	$20.00	$20.00	$20.00
Thermo Units	$100.00	$100.00	$100.00	$100.00	$100.00	$100.00	$100.00	$100.00	$100.00	$100.00	$100.00	$100.00
Heavy Equipment Glass	$100.00	$100.00	$100.00	$100.00	$100.00	$100.00	$100.00	$100.00	$100.00	$100.00	$100.00	$100.00
Ship Glass	$100.00	$100.00	$100.00	$100.00	$100.00	$100.00	$100.00	$100.00	$100.00	$100.00	$100.00	$100.00
Industrial Windshield Remove and Replace (Re/Re)	$50.00	$50.00	$50.00	$50.00	$50.00	$50.00	$50.00	$50.00	$50.00	$50.00	$50.00	$50.00
Sales Windshield	$0	$0	$0	$0	$0	$0	$0	$0	$0	$0	$0	$0

57

d Replacement ent												
Windshield Repair	$4,800	$4,800	$4,800	$4,800	$4,800	$4,800	$4,800	$4,800	$4,800	$4,800	$4,800	$4,800
	$0	$0	$0	$0	$0	$0	$0	$0	$0	$0	$0	$0
Tempered Glass (Back and Side)	$0	$0	$0	$0	$0	$0	$0	$0	$0	$0	$0	$0
Safety Glass And Plate Glass	$0	$0	$0	$0	$0	$0	$0	$0	$0	$0	$0	$0
Wipers	$0	$144	$144	$144	$144	$144	$144	$144	$144	$144	$144	$18
Aquapel	$40	$40	$40	$60	$60	$40	$40	$40	$40	$40	$40	$40
Thermo Units	$0	$0	$0	$0	$0	$0	$0	$0	$0	$0	$0	$0
Heavy Equipment Glass	$0	$0	$0	$0	$0	$0	$0	$0	$0	$0	$0	$0
Ship Glass	$0	$0	$0	$0	$0	$0	$0	$0	$0	$0	$0	$0
Industrial Windshield Remove and	$0	$0	$0	$0	$0	$0	$0	$0	$0	$0	$0	$0

	%	Month 1	Month 2	Month 3	Month 4	Month 5	Month 6	Month 7	Month 8	Month 9	Month 10	Month 11	Month 12
Replace (Re/Re) Total Sales		$4,840	$4,984	$4,984	$4,984	$5,004	$5,004	$4,984	$4,984	$4,984	$4,984	$4,984	$4,858
Direct Unit Costs													
Windshield	65.00%	$130.00	$130.00	$130.00	$130.00	$130.00	$130.00	$130.00	$130.00	$130.00	$130.00	$130.00	$130.00
Replacement Windshield Repair	8.00%	$6.40	$6.40	$6.40	$6.40	$6.40	$6.40	$6.40	$6.40	$6.40	$6.40	$6.40	$6.40
Tempered Glass (Back and Side)	65.00%	$97.50	$97.50	$97.50	$97.50	$97.50	$97.50	$97.50	$97.50	$97.50	$97.50	$97.50	$97.50
Safety Glass And Plate Glass	65.00%	$65.00	$65.00	$65.00	$65.00	$65.00	$65.00	$65.00	$65.00	$65.00	$65.00	$65.00	$65.00
Wipers	40.00%	$7.20	$7.20	$7.20	$7.20	$7.20	$7.20	$7.20	$7.20	$7.20	$7.20	$7.20	$7.20
Aquapel	10.00%	$2.00	$2.00	$2.00	$2.00	$2.00	$2.00	$2.00	$2.00	$2.00	$2.00	$2.00	$2.00

	%													
Thermo Units	65.00 %	$65.0	$65.0	$65.0	$65.0	$65.0	$65.0	$65.0	$65.0	$65.0	$65.0	$65.0	$65.0	$65.0
		0	0	0	0	0	0	0	0	0	0	0	0	0
Heavy Equipment Glass	65.00 %	$65.0	$65.0	$65.0	$65.0	$65.0	$65.0	$65.0	$65.0	$65.0	$65.0	$65.0	$65.0	$65.0
		0	0	0	0	0	0	0	0	0	0	0	0	0
Ship Glass Industrial	65.00 %	$65.0	$65.0	$65.0	$65.0	$65.0	$65.0	$65.0	$65.0	$65.0	$65.0	$65.0	$65.0	$65.0
		0	0	0	0	0	0	0	0	0	0	0	0	0
Windshield Remove and Replace (Re/Re)	20.00 %	$10.0	$10.0	$10.0	$10.0	$10.0	$10.0	$10.0	$10.0	$10.0	$10.0	$10.0	$10.0	$10.0
		0	0	0	0	0	0	0	0	0	0	0	0	0
Direct Cost of Sales														
Windshield Replacement		$0	$0	$0	$0	$0	$0	$0	$0	$0	$0	$0	$0	$0
Windshield Repair		$384	$384	$384	$384	$384	$384	$384	$384	$384	$384	$384	$384	$384
Tempered Glass		$0	$0	$0	$0	$0	$0	$0	$0	$0	$0	$0	$0	$0

(Back and Side)	$0	$0	$0	$0	$0	$0	$0	$0	$0	$0
Safety Glass And Plate Glass	$0	$0	$0	$0	$0	$0	$0	$0	$0	$0
Wipers	$0	$58	$58	$58	$58	$58	$58	$58	$58	$7
Aquapel	$4	$4	$4	$4	$6	$6	$4	$4	$4	$4
Thermo Units	$0	$0	$0	$0	$0	$0	$0	$0	$0	$0
Heavy Equipment Glass	$0	$0	$0	$0	$0	$0	$0	$0	$0	$0
Ship Glass	$0	$0	$0	$0	$0	$0	$0	$0	$0	$0
Industrial Windshield Remove and Replace (Re/Re)	$0	$0	$0	$0	$0	$0	$0	$0	$0	$0
Subtotal Direct Cost of Sales	$388	$446	$446	$446	$448	$448	$446	$446	$446	$446	$395

Personnel Plan	Month 1	Month 2	Month 3	Month 4	Month 5	Month 6	Month 7	Month 8	Month 9	Month 10	Month 11	Month 12
Andrew Wilstholm - Owner, Marketing & Sales	$1,200	$1,200	$1,200	$1,200	$1,200	$1,200	$1,200	$1,200	$1,200	$1,200	$1,200	$1,200
Part Timer - Unknow at this point	$0	$0	$0	$100	$800	$600	$1,000	$900	$1,200	$200	$0	$0
Total People	0	0	0	0	1	1	1	1	1	1	1	1
Total Payroll	$1,200	$1,200	$1,200	$1,300	$2,000	$1,800	$2,200	$2,100	$2,400	$1,400	$1,200	$1,200

Table: Profit and Loss

Pro Forma Profit and Loss	Month 1	Month 2	Month 3	Month 4	Month 5	Month 6	Month 7	Month 8	Month 9	Month 10	Month 11	Month 12
Sales	$4,840	$4,984	$4,982	$4,984	$5,004	$5,004	$4,984	$4,984	$4,984	$4,984	$4,984	$4,858
Direct Cost of Sales	$388	$446	$446	$446	$448	$448	$446	$446	$446	$446	$446	$395
Other Costs of Sales	$25	$25	$25	$25	$0	$25	$0	$25	$25	$0	$25	$0
Total Cost of Sales	$413	$471	$471	$471	$448	$473	$446	$471	$471	$446	$471	$395
Gross Margin	$4,427	$4,513	$4,512	$4,513	$4,556	$4,531	$4,538	$4,513	$4,513	$4,538	$4,513	$4,463
Gross Margin %	91.47%	90.56%	90.56%	90.56%	91.06%	90.56%	91.06%	90.56%	90.56%	91.06%	90.56%	91.86%
Expenses Payroll	$1,200	$1,200	$1,200	$1,300	$2,000	$1,800	$2,200	$2,100	$2,400	$1,400	$1,200	$1,200

Marketing/Promotion	$300	$300	$500	$300	$300	$300	$500	$300	$300	$300	$250	$300
Depreciation	$25	$25	$25	$25	$25	$25	$25	$25	$25	$25	$25	$25
Rent	$100	$100	$200	$300	$300	$300	$400	$300	$300	$300	$300	$400
Utilities	$100	$100	$100	$100	$100	$100	$100	$100	$100	$100	$100	$100
Insurance	$300	$300	$300	$300	$300	$300	$300	$300	$300	$300	$300	$300
Payroll Taxes (15%)	$180	$180	$180	$195	$300	$270	$330	$315	$360	$210	$180	$180
Other (15%)	$100	$100	$100	$100	$100	$110	$100	$0	$0	$0	$0	$0
Vehicle and Fuel (15%)	$200	$200	$200	$200	$300	$300	$300	$200	$200	$200	$200	$200
Phone and Internet	$100	$100	$100	$100	$100	$100	$100	$100	$100	$100	$100	$100
Total Operating Expenses	$2,605	$2,605	$2,905	$2,920	$3,825	$3,805	$4,355	$3,740	$4,085	$2,885	$2,705	$2,805
Profit Before Interest and Taxes	$1,822	$1,908	$1,608	$1,593	$731	$726	$183	$773	$428	$1,653	$1,808	$1,658
EBITDA	$1,847	$1,933	$1,633	$1,618	$756	$751	$208	$798	$453	$1,678	$1,833	$1,688
Interest Expense	$29	$28	$28	$28	$27	$27	$26	$26	$25	$25	$25	$25

Taxes Incurred	$538	$564	$474	$470	$211	$210	$47	$224	$121	$489	$535	$490
Net Profit	$1,255	$1,316	$1,105	$1,096	$493	$490	$110	$523	$282	$1,140	$1,249	$1,143
Net Profit/Sales	25.94%	26.41%	22.20%	21.99%	9.85%	9.79%	2.21%	10.50%	5.66%	22.87%	25.05%	23.53%

Table: Cash Flow

Pro Forma Cash Flow	Month 1	Month 2	Month 3	Month 4	Month 5	Month 6	Month 7	Month 8	Month 9	Month 10	Month 11	Month 12
Cash Received												
Cash from Operations												
Cash Sales	$3,630	$3,738	$3,738	$3,738	$3,753	$3,753	$3,738	$3,738	$3,738	$3,738	$3,738	$3,644
Cash from Receivables	$0	$645	$1,229	$1,246	$1,246	$1,249	$1,251	$1,248	$1,246	$1,246	$1,246	$1,246
Subtotal Cash from Operations	$3,630	$4,383	$4,967	$4,984	$4,999	$5,002	$4,989	$4,986	$4,984	$4,984	$4,984	$4,890
Additional Cash Received												
Sales Tax, VAT, 6.00%	$290	$299	$299	$299	$300	$300	$299	$299	$299	$299	$299	$291

HST/GST Received	$0	$0	$0	$0	$0	$0	$0	$0	$0	$0	$0	$0
New Current Borrowing	$2,000	$200	$1,000	$1,000	$1,000	$1,000	$1,000	$1,000	$1,000	$1,000	$1,000	$1,000
New Other Liabilities (interest-free)	$0	$0	$0	$0	$0	$0	$0	$0	$0	$0	$0	$0
New Long-term Liabilities	$0	$0	$0	$0	$0	$0	$0	$0	$0	$0	$0	$0
Sales of Other Current Assets	$0	$0	$0	$0	$0	$0	$0	$0	$0	$0	$0	$0
Sales of Long-term Assets	$0	$0	$0	$0	$0	$0	$0	$0	$0	$0	$0	$0
New Investment Received	$0	$0	$0	$0	$0	$0	$0	$0	$0	$0	$0	$0
Subtotal Cash	$5,920	$4,882	$6,266	$6,283	$6,299	$6,302	$6,288	$6,285	$6,283	$6,283	$6,283	$6,181

	Month 1	Month 2	Month 3	Month 4	Month 5	Month 6	Month 7	Month 8	Month 9	Month 10	Month 11	Month 12
Received												
Expenditures												
Expenditures from Operations												
Cash Spending	$1,200	$1,200	$1,200	$1,300	$2,000	$1,800	$2,200	$2,100	$2,400	$1,400	$1,200	$1,200
Bill Payments	$879	$2,362	$2,450	$2,650	$2,560	$2,493	$2,688	$2,639	$2,334	$2,282	$2,422	$2,510
Subtotal Spent on Operations	$2,079	$3,562	$3,650	$3,950	$4,560	$4,293	$4,888	$4,739	$4,734	$3,682	$3,622	$3,710
Additional Cash Spent												
Sales Tax, VAT, HST/GST Paid Out	$290	$299	$299	$299	$300	$300	5$0	$299	$299	$299	$299	$291
Principal Repayment	$50	$50	$50	$50	$50	$50	$299	$50	$50	$50	$50	$0

of Current Borrowing	$25	$0	$0	$0	$0	$0	$0	$0	$0	$0	$0	$0
Other Liabilities Principal Repayment	$0	$0	$0	$0	$0	$0	$0	$0	$0	$0	$0	$0
Long-term Liabilities Principal Repayment	$0	$0	$0	$0	$0	$0	$0	$0	$0	$0	$0	$0
Purchase Other Current Assets	$50	$0	$0	$0	$0	$0	$0	$0	$0	$0	$0	$0
Purchase Long-term Assets	$0	$0	$0	$0	$0	$0	$0	$0	$0	$0	$0	$0
Dividends	$0	$0	$0	$0	$0	$0	$0	$0	$0	$0	$0	$0
Subtotal Cash Spent	$2,494	$3,912	$3,999	$4,299	$4,911	$4,643	$5,237	$5,088	$5,083	$4,031	$3,971	$4,001
Net Cash Flow	$3,426	$971	$2,267	$1,984	$1,389	$1,659	$1,051	$1,198	$1,200	$2,252	$2,312	$2,180
Cash Balance	$4,426	$5,397	$7,664	$9,649	$11,037	$12,696	$13,748	$14,945	$16,146	$18,398	$20,710	$22,890

Table: Balance Sheet

Pro Forma Balance Sheet	Starting Balances	Month 1	Month 2	Month 3	Month 4	Month 5	Month 6	Month 7	Month 8	Month 9	Month 10	Month 11	Month 12
Assets													
Current Assets													
Cash	$1,000	$4,426	$5,397	$7,664	$9,649	$11,037	$12,696	$13,748	$14,945	$16,146	$18,398	$20,710	$22,890
Accounts Receivable	$0	$1,210	$1,811	$1,827	$1,827	$1,832	$1,835	$1,830	$1,827	$1,827	$1,827	$1,827	$1,796
Other Current Assets	$0	$50	$50	$50	$50	$50	$50	$50	$50	$50	$50	$50	$50
Total	$1,000	$5,68	$7,25	$9,54	$11,5	$12,9	$14,5	$15,6	$16,8	$18,0	$20,2	$22,5	$24,7

		Month 1	Month 2	Month 3	Month 4	Month 5	Month 6	Month 7	Month 8	Month 9	Month 10	Month 11	Month 12
Current Assets	$1,000	$5,686	$7,258	$9,542	$11,526	$12,920	$14,581	$15,627	$16,823	$18,023	$20,275	$22,587	$24,736
Long-term Assets	$2,850	$2,850	$2,850	$2,850	$2,850	$2,850	$2,850	$2,850	$2,850	$2,850	$2,850	$2,850	$2,850
Accumulated Depreciation	$0	$25	$50	$75	$100	$125	$150	$175	$200	$225	$250	$275	$300
Total Long-term Assets	$2,850	$2,825	$2,800	$2,775	$2,750	$2,725	$2,700	$2,675	$2,650	$2,625	$2,600	$2,575	$2,550
Total Assets	$3,850	$8,511	$10,058	$12,317	$14,276	$15,645	$17,281	$18,302	$19,473	$20,648	$22,875	$25,162	$27,286
Liabilities and Capital													
Current													

Liabilities													
Accounts Payable	$800	$2,281	$2,362	$2,564	$2,477	$2,403	$2,600	$2,561	$2,258	$2,201	$2,338	$2,427	$2,407
Current Borrowing	$1,000	$950	$900	$850	$800	$750	$700	$650	$600	$550	$500	$450	$450
Other Current Liabilities	$200	$2,175	$2,375	$3,375	$4,375	$5,375	$6,375	$7,375	$8,375	$9,375	$10,375	$11,375	$12,375
Subtotal Current Liabilities	$2,000	$5,406	$5,637	$6,789	$7,652	$8,528	$9,675	$10,586	$11,233	$12,126	$13,213	$14,252	$15,232
Long-term Liabilities	$2,500	$2,500	$2,500	$2,500	$2,500	$2,500	$2,500	$2,500	$2,500	$2,500	$2,500	$2,500	$2,500
Total Liabilities	$4,500	$7,906	$8,137	$9,289	$10,152	$11,028	$12,175	$13,086	$13,733	$14,626	$15,713	$16,752	$17,732
Paid-in Capital	$500	$500	$500	$500	$500	$500	$500	$500	$500	$500	$500	$500	$500
Retained Earnings	($1,150)	($1,150)	($1,150)	($1,150)	($1,150)	($1,150)	($1,150)	($1,150)	($1,150)	($1,150)	($1,150)	($1,150)	($1,150)
Earnings	$0	$1,255	$2,571	$3,678	$4,774	$5,267	$5,757	$5,867	$6,397	$6,672	$7,812	$9,061	$10,204

Total Capital	($650)	$605	$1,921	$3,028	$4,124	$4,617	$5,107	$5,217	$5,740	$6,022	$7,162	$8,411	$9,554
Total Liabilities and Capital	$3,850	$8,511	$10,058	$12,317	$14,276	$15,645	$17,281	$18,302	$19,473	$20,648	$22,875	$25,162	$27,286
Net Worth	($650)	$605	$1,921	$3,028	$4,124	$4,617	$5,107	$5,217	$5,740	$6,022	$7,162	$8,411	$9,554

Additional Resources

United States

- Small Business Administration -
  http://www.sba.gov/category/navigation-structure/starting-managing-business

Canada

- Atlantic Canada Opportunities Agency - http://www.acoa-apeca.gc.ca/eng/IWantTo/StartABusiness/Pages/Home.aspx

- Canada Business - http://www.canadabusiness.ca/eng/

Resources by Automotive Marketing Blueprint

http://www.automotivemarketingblueprint.com/

Forming Strategies
For the
Sales Approach
Automotive Marketing Blueprint

WINDSHIELD REPAIR
MARKETING
SUCCESS SYSTEM

Insurance Intelligence
Your Starting Platform
Automotive Marketing Blueprint
Insurance Intelligence

WINDSHIELD REPAIR
MARKETING
SUCCESS SYSTEM

LEGAL
DOCUMENTS
Your Starting Platform
Automotive Marketing Blueprint

WINDSHIELD REPAIR
MARKETING
SUCCESS SYSTEM

Automotive Marketing Blueprint
Automotive Marketing Blueprint
Automotive Marketing Blueprint
Windshield Repair Technical Manual

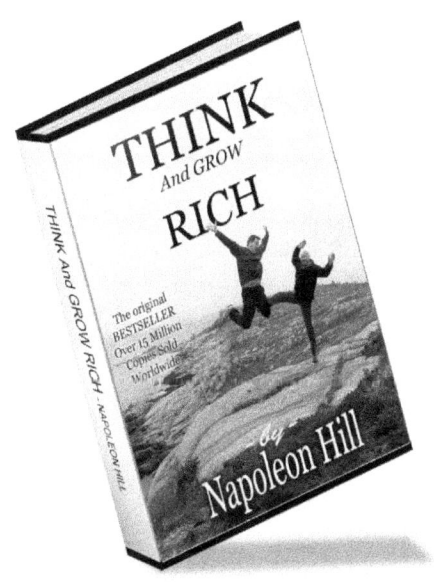

Confidentiality Agreement

The undersigned reader acknowledges that the information provided by
_____ in this business plan is confidential; therefore, reader
agrees not to disclose it without the express written permission of
_____.

It is acknowledged by reader that information to be furnished in this
business plan is in all respects confidential in nature, other than information
which is in the public domain through other means and that any disclosure
or use of same by reader may cause serious harm or damage to
_____.

Upon request, this document is to be immediately returned to
_____.

_____
Signature

_____
Name (typed or printed)

_____
Date

This is a business plan. It does not imply an offering of securities.

ABOUT THE AUTHOR

Andrew AJ Wilstholm (Bcomm in Marketing and HR professional) was born and raised in Mount Uniacke, Nova Scotia. Wilstholm is a serial entrepreneur and enjoys creating businesses and helping other small businesses succeed. Wilstholm has been in the auto glass trade since 1985 where his first job was to deliver flyer and sell the business. Wilstholm owned his first auto glass business in 1996 and eventually sold it for profit and the company with a solid foundation still thriving today. In 2008 he completed his business degree from Saint Mary's University. Wilstholm is active on the Nova Scotia Automotive Apprentice Board for developing training materials, educational products and the further development of the automotive glass trade in Atlantic Canada. In his spare time he enjoys spending time with family, the outdoors, like summiting Mount Katahdin or Gros Morne mountain, hunting, fishing and completed his first Ironman in Mont Tremblant, Quebec. Enjoying Life

www.ingramcontent.com/pod-product-compliance
Lightning Source LLC
Chambersburg PA
CBHW071255170526
45165CB00003B/1358